DR JEKYLL AND MR HYDE: 12 AQA GCSE ENGLISH LITERATURE A STAR EXAM ANSWERS

Full mark A Star (Grade 9) Answers

By Joseph Anthony Campbell

Copyright © 2022 by Joseph Anthony Campbell. All Rights Reserved.

All rights reserved. No part of this book may be reproduced in any form or by any electronic or mechanical means including information storage and retrieval systems, without permission in writing from the author.

First Printing: September 2022

For all professional enquiries, I can be contacted via email at
Joseph@agradeexams.com

DR JEKYLL AND MR HYDE: 12 AQA GCSE ENGLISH LITERATURE A STAR EXAM ANSWERS

CONTENTS

CONTENTS 1
The Quality Control System™ or how to get an A star!...2
AQA English Literature GCSE - Dr. Jekyll and Mr. Hyde Format..3
Dr. Jekyll and Mr. Hyde First Essay – Mr. Utterson 4
Dr. Jekyll and Mr. Hyde Second Essay – Mr. Hyde as a Frightening Outsider...........................8
Dr. Jekyll and Mr. Hyde Third Essay – The Relationship between Dr. Jekyll and Mr. Utterson...12
Dr. Jekyll and Mr. Hyde Fourth Essay – Mr. Hyde as a Terrifying Figure 16
Dr. Jekyll and Mr. Hyde Fifth Essay – The Themes of Mystery and Tension 20
Dr. Jekyll and Mr. Hyde Sixth Essay – The Relationship between Mr. Utterson and Dr. Lanyon...24
Dr. Jekyll and Mr. Hyde Seventh Essay - Stevenson's Presentation of Dr. Jekyll 28
Dr. Jekyll and Mr. Hyde Eighth Essay – Mr. Hyde as Inhuman and Disturbing........................32
Dr. Jekyll and Mr. Hyde Ninth Essay – The Relationship between Mr. Hyde/Dr. Jekyll and Dr. Lanyon 36
Dr. Jekyll and Mr. Hyde Tenth Essay – Dr. Lanyon..40
Dr. Jekyll and Mr. Hyde Eleventh Essay – Stevenson's Presentation of Dr. Jekyll as Conflicted 44
Dr. Jekyll and Mr. Hyde Twelfth Essay – The Themes of Good and Evil 48
Assessment Objectives 52
Timings 54
Approximate Word Count Per Question 55
Author's Note..56
About the Author 57
Limited availability for online and in person (in London) GCSE ENGLISH tuition with me........58

By Joseph Anthony Campbell

THE QUALITY CONTROL SYSTEM™ OR HOW TO GET AN A STAR!

The Quality Control System™ is fourfold.

It involves:

1) An efficient summary of the examination paper.

2) A concise focus upon the Assessment Objectives in the exam and how to approach them.

3) Clear instructions on your timings and how long you should spend on each question. ***This is the most important point of fact in this fourfold system***.

4) Further to point 3, the approximate word count per mark you should be consistently aiming for in each minute of your exam.

My students have applied all of the techniques of the Quality Control System™ I am providing you with to gain A stars (Grade 9's) in their examinations. You can replicate them by following the advice in this book. Following these rules has ensured success for my students in English Literature and their other subjects and it will do for you too! The Quality Control System is explained more fully at the end of this book.

AQA ENGLISH LITERATURE GCSE – DR. JEKYLL AND MR. HYDE FORMAT

19th-century novel – 1 item. 30 marks (AO1, AO2, AO3)

We are looking in this book at the '**19th-century novel**' section and the '**The Strange Case of Dr. Jekyll and Mr. Hyde**' option. There are 12 examples of Grade 9, A star essays in this book. There will be one question on each nineteenth century novel. In each question there will be a short extract from the novel and you will be required to write on the extract and to widen your response to the novel as a whole.

The following 12 questions and answers will help you to prepare your Grade 9 essays and to massively improve your practice for your exams as I have covered all of the major characters in '**The Strange Case of Dr. Jekyll and Mr. Hyde**' in this book and the major themes.

The best approach for a **Grade 9** is to spend 50 minutes on each question; 40 minutes writing and 10 minutes making notes, planning and checking your final answer for basic corrections at the end of the examination!

This series of books have helped thousands of readers to achieve their potential!

By Joseph Anthony Campbell

DR. JEKYLL AND MR. HYDE FIRST ESSAY – MR. UTTERSON

Read the following extract from Chapter 1 and then answer the question that follows.

In this extract, Mr. Utterson is being introduced by Stevenson, at the very beginning of the novel.

Mr. Utterson the lawyer was a man of a rugged countenance, that was never lighted by a smile; cold, scanty and embarrassed in discourse; backward in sentiment; lean, long, dusty, dreary and yet somehow lovable. At friendly meetings, and when the wine was to his taste, something eminently human beaconed from his eye; something indeed which never found its way into his talk, but which spoke not only in these silent symbols of the after-dinner face, but more often and loudly in the acts of his life. He was austere with himself; drank gin when he was alone, to mortify a taste for vintages; and though he enjoyed the theatre, had not crossed the doors of one for twenty years. But he had an approved tolerance for others; sometimes wondering, almost with envy, at the high pressure of spirits involved in their misdeeds; and in any extremity inclined to help rather than to reprove. "I incline to Cain's heresy," he used to say quaintly: "I let my brother go to the devil in his own way." In this character, it was frequently his fortune to be the last reputable acquaintance and the last good influence in the lives of down-going men. And to such as these, so long as they came about his chambers, he never marked a shade of change in his demeanour. No doubt the feat was easy to Mr. Utterson; for he was undemonstrative at the best, and even his friendships seemed to be founded in a similar catholicity of good-nature.

It is the mark of a modest man to accept his friendly circle ready-made from the hands of opportunity; and that was the lawyer's way. His friends were those of his own blood or those whom he had known the longest; his affections, like ivy, were the growth of time, they implied no aptness in the object.

Starting with this extract, how does Stevenson present Mr. Utterson?

Write about:

• *how Stevenson presents Mr. Utterson in this extract*
• *how Stevenson presents Mr. Utterson in the novel as a whole.*

[30 marks] (AO1 = 12; AO2 = 12; AO3 = 6)

(50 Minutes Total = 40 Minutes Writing + 10 Minutes Reading Extract/Making Notes/Planning)

(600 Words Maximum per Essay = 15 Words per Minute)

In this extract, Stevenson presents the character of Mr. Utterson, a London lawyer. Stevenson states that, "He was austere with himself;" yet "…something eminently human beaconed from his eye." Utterson is both measured and emotionless yet nevertheless he has an "…approved tolerance for others" and he is "…inclined to help rather than to reprove." From the description provided by Stevenson in this extract, Utterson appears to be both trustworthy and tolerant of the faults of others. He has a profound respect for his fellow man and he is often found to be the final remaining friend and "…the last good influence in the lives of down-going men." Utterson is "modest" also as "His friends were those of his own blood or those whom he had known the longest; his affections, like ivy, were the growth of time,". Stevenson uses Mr. Utterson as the main protagonist throughout the novella and even states that he is "lovable". He is a pivotal character that drives the plot and he is involved in many of the most dramatic and structurally significant moments of the novella.

Throughout the novella Stevenson presents Mr. Utterson as a loyal and close friend of both Dr. Jekyll and Dr. Lanyon. Utterson is a respectable, wealthy lawyer in Victorian London. Stevenson shows Utterson's personality to be rational, calm and curious. However, although he states of Utterson that "…few men could read the rolls of their life with less apprehension" he also juxtaposes this with the words that Utterson, "…was humbled to the dust by the many ill things he had done". Most of the novella is observed from Mr Utterson's perspective through Stevenson's use of a third person narrative structure.

Utterson exhibits both curiosity and persistence in his quest to uncover the true reality of Mr. Hyde and his relationship with Dr. Jekyll. "If he be Mr. Hyde," he had thought, "I shall be Mr. Seek." His friends also hold him in high esteem as when he views Dr. Jekyll from his window, Dr. Jekyll states to Utterson, "'I am very glad to see you; this is really a great pleasure;'" and Utterson is accommodating of his friends' needs, "'Why then,' said the lawyer good-naturedly, "the best thing we can do is to stay down here and speak with you from where we are.'" His close bonds have been forged through time with Dr. Jekyll and Dr. Lanyon from the "…old days when the trio were inseparable friends."

Later in the novella, Utterson's calm, good sense and rational disposition brings relief to Dr. Jekyll's staff. His sense of righteousness and integrity counteracts the evil anguish and despair that Jekyll's staff have been unfairly subjected to for a prolonged period of time, through Mr. Hyde. Stevenson states, "At the sight of Mr. Utterson, the house-maid broke into hysterical whimpering; and the cook, crying out 'Bless God! it's Mr. Utterson,' ran forward as if to take him in her arms." Utterson also acts despite his fear and "…recollected his courage" before his final dramatic meeting with the now inseparable Dr. Jekyll and Mr. Hyde; which further endears him to readers.

The dramatic context and spectacle of Stevenson's novella would have been greatly enjoyed during the Victorian era. In this gothic tale, a sinister, mysterious atmosphere is often prevalent and Utterson acts as a contrast to Mr. Hyde's dark acts and behaviour. A created character is never entirely separate from the author and Utterson perhaps reflects Stevenson's nature, as perhaps does Mr. Hyde. Through the contrast of both light and dark elements throughout the story; Stevenson creates an intertwining and dramatically effective metaphor.

(600 words)

DR. JEKYLL AND MR. HYDE SECOND ESSAY – MR. HYDE AS A FRIGHTENING OUTSIDER

Read the following extract from Chapter 2 and then answer the question that follows.

In this extract Mr. Utterson has just met Mr. Hyde for the first time.

"We have common friends," said Mr. Utterson.
"Common friends!" echoed Mr. Hyde, a little hoarsely. "Who are they?"
"Jekyll, for instance," said the lawyer.
"He never told you," cried Mr. Hyde, with a flush of anger. "I did not think you
5 would have lied."
"Come," said Mr. Utterson, "that is not fitting language."
The other snarled aloud into a savage laugh; and the next moment, with extraordinary quickness, he had unlocked the door and disappeared into the house.
10 The lawyer stood awhile when Mr. Hyde had left him, the picture of disquietude. Then he began slowly to mount the street, pausing every step or two and putting his hand to his brow like a man in mental perplexity. The problem he was thus debating as he walked was one of a class that is rarely solved. Mr. Hyde was pale and dwarfish; he gave an impression of deformity
15 without any nameable malformation, he had a displeasing smile, he had borne himself to the lawyer with a sort of murderous mixture of timidity and

boldness, and he spoke with a husky whispering and somewhat broken voice, – all these were points against him; but not all of these together could explain the hitherto unknown disgust, loathing and fear with which Mr. Utterson
20 regarded him. "There must be something else," said the perplexed gentleman. "There is something more, if I could find a name for it. God bless me, the man seems hardly human! Something troglodytic, shall we say? Or can it be the old story of Dr. Fell? Or is it the mere radiance of a foul soul that thus transpires through, and transfigures, its clay continent? The last, I think;
25 for, O my poor old Harry Jekyll, if ever I read Satan's signature upon a face, it is on that of your new friend!"

Starting with this extract, how does Stevenson present Mr. Hyde as a frightening outsider?

Write about:

• *how Stevenson presents Mr. Hyde in this extract*
• *how Stevenson presents Mr. Hyde as a frightening outsider in the novel as a whole.*

[30 marks] (AO1 = 12; AO2 = 12; AO3 = 6)

(50 Minutes Total = 40 Minutes Writing + 10 Minutes Reading Extract/Making Notes/Planning)

(600 Words Maximum per Essay = 15 Words per Minute)

Stevenson presents Mr. Hyde in this extract as the impersonal "other" as he "...snarled aloud into a savage laugh; and ...with extraordinary quickness, ...disappeared". Mr. Hyde's actions appear inhuman and this is further exemplified by the words that Stevenson uses to describe Mr. Hyde's physical appearance and behaviour. Hyde is described as "pale and dwarfish;" and that "he gave an impression of deformity" yet even this has the mysterious effect of not being a "nameable malformation,". Even Mr. Hyde's "smile," which is traditionally associated with being socially pleasant, is "displeasing". Stevenson describes Hyde through the alliteration of having a "murderous mixture" of the starkly contrasting qualities of "timidity and boldness,". It is clear here that Mr. Hyde is presented as being both frightening and an outsider.

Stevenson uses a triplet to describe Mr. Utterson's reactions to Mr. Hyde, as he has a level of "disgust, loathing and fear" which had been "hitherto unknown" to him. Utterson's generally emotionless nature and the unknown and unusual shock and confusion that he experiences upon meeting Mr. Hyde, leads him to a series of questions that he asks himself aloud. This is in order to understand his intense reactions to Mr. Hyde and he finally deduces that, "'the man seems hardly human! Something troglodytic'". The word 'troglodytic' is an interesting use of language by Stevenson as Victorian society at this time had only recently been exposed to Darwin's evolutionary ideas. However, Stevenson, through the character of Utterson, returns to a more contemporary religious understanding of Hyde's nature, "'…if ever I read Satan's signature upon a face,'".

Stevenson presents Mr. Hyde as a frightening outsider throughout the novella as a whole and there is a build-up of dramatic tension prior to this extract. Utterson is first introduced to the name "Hyde" as Enfield recounts of Hyde that he "'…trampled calmly over the child's body and left her'". Later in his story, he states that when Hyde was surrounded by "'hateful faces'", he was "'in the middle, with a kind of black, sneering coolness" and "carrying it off, …really like Satan.". Hyde is certainly frightening and he is outside of normal human society, as here he is both physically and mentally isolated from others. Hyde's frightening and demonic aspects are also again accentuated by Stevenson's reference to Hyde's similarity to "Satan" both here and in the extract. In Victorian society, "'like Satan'" would have been a powerful and fearful simile to use, as there was a much stronger belief in 'Satan' than can be found contemporarily.

Enfield further re-iterates the sense of Hyde's appearance being both frightening and outside of and apart from, normal humanity, when he states, "'There is something wrong with his appearance; something displeasing, something downright detestable. I never saw a man I so disliked,". Hyde is certainly outside of the reputable society of Victorian London and the repetition and use of the triplet of the word 'something' by Enfield, accentuates the mysterious, dark qualities of Mr. Hyde.

Hyde is presented by Stevenson as an alienated figure, isolated from others. He is also a frightening outsider as whenever other people observe him, they are deeply and negatively affected by his looks and spirit. Hyde's behaviour and actions are clearly outside of the prevailing social attitudes of the Victorian era. As a literary character, Hyde is clearly aligned with the gothic genre that Stevenson writes in, as he is sinister, grotesque and mysterious. The dramatic context and spectacle of Hyde as a frightening outsider is demonstrated by Stevenson throughout the novella and through how other characters react to the very essence of his being.

(600 words)

DR. JEKYLL AND MR. HYDE THIRD ESSAY – THE RELATIONSHIP BETWEEN DR. JEKYLL AND MR. UTTERSON

Read the following extract from Chapter 3 and then answer the question that follows.

In this extract Mr. Utterson and Dr. Jekyll discuss the relationship between Dr. Jekyll and Mr. Hyde.

The large handsome face of Dr. Jekyll grew pale to the very lips, and there came a blackness about his eyes. "I do not care to hear more," said he. "This is a matter I thought we had agreed to drop."
"What I heard was abominable," said Utterson.
"It can make no change. You do not understand my position," returned the doctor, with a certain incoherency of manner. "I am painfully situated, Utterson; my position is a very strange—a very strange one. It is one of those affairs that cannot be mended by talking."
"Jekyll," said Utterson, "you know me: I am a man to be trusted. Make a clean breast of this in confidence; and I make no doubt I can get you out of it."
"My good Utterson," said the doctor, "this is very good of you, this is downright good of you, and I cannot find words to thank you in. I believe you fully; I would trust you

before any man alive, ay, before myself, if I could make the choice; but indeed it isn't what you fancy; it is not so bad as that; and just to put your good heart at rest, I will tell you one thing: the moment I choose, I can be rid of Mr. Hyde. I give you my hand upon that; and I thank you again and again; and I will just add one little word, Utterson, that I'm sure you'll take in good part: this is a private matter, and I beg of you to let it sleep."

Utterson reflected a little looking in the fire.

"I have no doubt you are perfectly right," he said at last, getting to his feet.

"Well, but since we have touched upon this business, and for the last time I hope," continued the doctor, "there is one point I should like you to understand. I have really a very great interest in poor Hyde. I know you have seen him; he told me so; and I fear he was rude. But I do sincerely take a great, a very great interest in that young man; and if I am taken away, Utterson, I wish you to promise me that you will bear with him and get his rights for him. I think you would, if you knew all; and it would be a weight off my mind if you would promise."

"I can't pretend that I shall ever like him," said the lawyer.

"I don't ask that," pleaded Jekyll, laying his hand upon the other's arm; "I only ask for justice; I only ask you to help him for my sake, when I am no longer here."

Utterson heaved an irrepressible sigh. "Well," said he. "I promise."

Starting with this extract, how does Stevenson present the relationship between Dr. Jekyll and Mr. Utterson?

Write about:

• how Stevenson presents their relationship in this extract
• how Stevenson presents the relationship between Dr. Jekyll and Mr. Utterson in the novel as a whole.

[30 marks] (AO1 = 12; AO2 = 12; AO3 = 6)

(50 Minutes Total = 40 Minutes Writing + 10 Minutes Reading Extract/Making Notes/Planning)

(600 Words Maximum per Essay = 15 Words per Minute)

In this extract, Stevenson presents Mr. Utterson as concerned, as he mentions the fact of Jekyll changing his will and leaving everything to Hyde. Jekyll aims to allay Utterson's worries and asks him to mention the matter no more. However, there is a close bond between Mr. Utterson and Dr. Jekyll that has been formed over many years, as demonstrated when Utterson appeals to Jekyll stating, "'you know me: I am a man to be trusted.'" Mr. Utterson admires, values and cares for his friend, Dr. Jekyll. The close bond is reciprocated as Dr. Jekyll appreciates his friend's kind offer and he is grateful for his friendship. "'This is very good of you, ...and I cannot find words to thank you in.'" It is clear, however, that the relationship between Dr. Jekyll and Mr. Hyde is more complicated than Mr. Utterson suspects, when Jekyll states, "I do sincerely take a great, a very great interest in that young man." The repetition of 'great' emphasises and reinforces how determined Jekyll is to protect Mr. Hyde's interests with the use of the word 'sincerely' adding an extra layer of authenticity to his words.

It is interesting to note, however, that Utterson remains unmoved as regards his feelings for Mr. Hyde, stating, "'I can't pretend that I shall ever like him,'". This reflects Utterson's integrity and honesty as he states his true feelings despite his close friendship with Jekyll. However, Utterson still acquiesces to his friend Jekyll's request for 'justice', relenting and replying, "'I promise.'". The intention and motivations behind Jekyll's speech and actions later reveal a hidden subtext.

Stevenson presents the relationship between Dr. Jekyll and Mr. Utterson throughout the novella. Immediately prior to the extract, Stevenson states of Dr. Jekyll that, "...you could see by his looks that he cherished for Mr. Utterson a sincere and warm affection." When Utterson meets Hyde, his main concern is for the welfare of his friend as he states, "'O my poor old Harry Jekyll,'". However, as Dr. Jekyll retreats into isolation, the relationship between Utterson and Jekyll changes, as Utterson, still, "...thought of him kindly; but his thoughts were disquieted and fearful" and that eventually he "...fell off little by little in the frequency of his visits." Later in the novella, as Utterson notices Jekyll at his window, he kindly implores, "'Come now; get your hat and take a quick turn with us.'" and the affection is returned by Jekyll who states in a bittersweet fashion, "'You are very good,' sighed the other." This, however, is the last time Utterson is to see Dr. Jekyll alive.

Utterson is the first person "...to receive a visit from Poole", (Jekyll's servant) and when he hears of potential grievous danger to Dr. Jekyll, "Mr. Utterson's only answer was to rise and get his hat and great coat;". Utterson receives the last words of Jekyll, who is now permanently transformed to his alter-ego Mr. Hyde: "'Utterson,'... 'for God's sake, have mercy!'" and ironically his great friend precipitates Jekyll's suicide as he replies, "'Ah, that's not Jekyll's voice—it's Hyde's!'... 'Down with the door, Poole.'" Their close relationship is fully confirmed as Utterson receives Jekyll's "...deed of gift in case of disappearance;" and the "...confession of, 'Your unworthy and unhappy friend, 'Henry Jekyll.'"

Stevenson uses both Dr. Jekyll and Mr. Utterson to influence the plot's development, as each are pivotal characters that drive the plot. In terms of the dramatic context - the spectacle would have been enjoyed during the Victorian era, as would Stevenson's presentation of a sinister and mysterious atmosphere; a key feature of the gothic genre.

(600 words)

By Joseph Anthony Campbell

DR. JEKYLL AND MR. HYDE FOURTH ESSAY – MR. HYDE AS A TERRIFYING FIGURE

Read the following extract from Chapter 4 and then answer the question that follows.

In this extract, we are given the maid's perspective of the murder of Sir Danvers Carew.

And as she so sat she became aware of an aged and beautiful gentleman with white hair, drawing near along the lane; and advancing to meet him, another and very small gentleman, to whom at first she paid less attention. When they had come within speech (which was just under the maid's eyes) the older man bowed and accosted the other with a very pretty manner of politeness. It did not seem as if the subject of his address were of great importance; indeed, from his pointing, it sometimes appeared as if he were only inquiring his way; but the moon shone on his face as he spoke, and the girl was pleased to watch it, it seemed to breathe such an innocent and old-world kindness of disposition, yet with, something high too, as of a well-founded self-content. Presently her eye wandered to the other, and she was surprised to recognise in him a certain Mr. Hyde, who had once visited her master and for whom she had conceived a dislike. He had in his hand a heavy cane, with which he was trifling; but he answered never a word, and seemed to listen with an ill-contained impatience. And then all of a sudden he broke out in a great flame of anger, stamping with his foot, brandishing the cane, and carrying on (as the maid described it) like a madman. The old gentleman took a step back, with the air of one very much surprised and a trifle hurt; and at that Mr. Hyde broke out of all bounds and clubbed him to the earth. And next moment, with ape-like fury, he was trampling his victim under foot, and hailing down a storm of blows, under which the bones were audibly shattered and the body jumped upon the roadway. At the horror of these sights and sounds, the maid fainted.

Starting with this extract, how does Stevenson present Mr. Hyde as a terrifying figure?

Write about:

* *how Stevenson presents Mr. Hyde in this extract*
* *how Stevenson presents Mr. Hyde as a terrifying figure in the novel as a whole.*

[30 marks] (AO1 = 12; AO2 = 12; AO3 = 6)

(50 Minutes Total = 40 Minutes Writing + 10 Minutes Reading Extract/Making Notes/Planning)

(600 Words Maximum per Essay = 15 Words per Minute)

Stevenson presents Mr. Hyde in this extract as he is driven to attack and murder Sir Danvers Carew an "…aged and beautiful gentleman with white hair" without any apparent cause. The maid witnesses Hyde murder Carew with Jekyll's cane and his feet in a murderous rage. She describes Hyde as someone "…for whom she had conceived a dislike" and this is a key feature of descriptions of Hyde, as all who meet Hyde in the novella are afflicted by his appearance and by something unnameable and disturbing. In this extract, Hyde "…answered never a word" and had "an ill-contained impatience" before "he broke out in a great flame of anger". This symbolises the terrifying and sudden nature of Hyde's 'anger' in this extract, as he acted, "like a madman".

Stevenson presents Hyde at his most terrifying as he "broke out of all bounds, and clubbed him to the earth." The use of the verb 'clubbed' demonstrates the brutality of Mr. Hyde and, "...with ape-like fury, he was trampling his victim under foot, and hailing down a storm of blows." The use of the simile 'ape-like fury' also describes Hyde's animalistic, inhumane behaviour. Stevenson uses onomatopoeia through words such as "stamping", "trampling" and "shattered". Hyde's "stamping" shows the viciousness and vindictiveness of his attack and the word "trampling" describes the sound of his stamping as "the bones were audibly shattered." Stevenson's use of language allows the reader to imagine the sound of Carew's bones breaking and to clearly picture the brutality of the murder. Stevenson's use of fearful images and sounds presents the terrifying and vicious, true nature of Mr. Hyde to the reader.

Stevenson presents Mr. Hyde as a terrifying figure who commits horrific acts throughout the novella. Following the extract, Stevenson describes "The stick with which the deed had been done ...had broken under the stress of this insensate cruelty;". The cane Hyde uses as a murder weapon has 'broken' from the murderous force applied to it. Stevenson uses a powerful verb when describing Carew's dead body, stating that it is "mangled." Sir Danvers Carew is now an unidentifiable, 'mangled' body through the terrifying actions of Mr. Hyde.

Throughout the novella, Hyde commits wild acts of violence against innocent people such as the young girl he "trampled" on. Hyde also inspires terror in those he encounters. Dr. Lanyon experiences his "...mind submerged in terror" after he witnesses Hyde's transformation into Dr. Jekyll which results in a "...deep-seated terror of the mind" which ultimately results in Lanyon's death. As Utterson and Enfield are talking to Dr. Jekyll and he becomes aware of his impending, unexpected transformation, "an expression of such abject terror and despair as froze the very blood of the two gentlemen below" appears upon Jekyll's face. Also, when Poole visits Utterson he "first announced his terror" of the person (Hyde) who now resides in Jekyll's cabinet. Later, when Hyde is finally confronted, Stevenson states that Hyde produces "A dismal screech, as of mere animal terror,". Dr. Jekyll also describes the murder of Danvers Carew while he was transformed into Hyde and states that "I mauled the unresisting body, tasting delight from every blow;".

Throughout the novella, Hyde's appearance and actions inspire terror in others. Stevenson writes in the gothic genre, which originated in the 18th century and describes sinister, grotesque, mysterious and dark characters as embodied by the terrifying figure of Mr. Hyde. To murder a human being is to break the 'Ten Commandments' – according to a religious Victorian readership and murder is something that a contemporary, modern-day audience would think of as evil and terrifying also.

(600 words)

By Joseph Anthony Campbell

DR. JEKYLL AND MR. HYDE FIFTH ESSAY – THE THEMES OF MYSTERY AND TENSION

Read the following extract from Chapter 4 (The Carew Murder Case) of <u>The Strange Case of Dr. Jekyll and Mr. Hyde</u> and then answer the question that follows.

In this extract, Utterson and Inspector Newcomen have come to find Mr. Hyde at his lodging house after the murder of Sir Danvers Carew.

It was by this time about nine in the morning, and the first fog of the season. A great chocolate-coloured pall lowered over heaven, but the wind was continually charging and routing these embattled vapours; so that as the cab crawled from street to street, Mr. Utterson beheld a marvellous number of degrees and hues of
5 twilight; for here it would be dark like the back-end of evening; and there would be a glow of a rich, lurid brown, like the light of some strange conflagration; and here, for a moment, the fog would be quite broken up, and a haggard shaft of daylight would glance in between the swirling wreaths. The dismal quarter of Soho seen under these changing glimpses, with its muddy ways, and slatternly
10 passengers, and its lamps, which had never been extinguished or had been kindled afresh to combat this mournful re-invasion of darkness, seemed, in the lawyer's eyes, like a district of some city in a nightmare.
The thoughts of his mind, besides, were of the gloomiest dye; and when he

glanced at the companion of his drive, he was conscious of some touch of that *15* terror of the law and the law's officers which may at times assail the most honest. As the cab drew up before the address indicated, the fog lifted a little, and showed him a dingy street, a gin-palace, a low French eating-house, a shop for the retail of penny numbers and twopenny salads, many ragged children huddled in the doorways, and many women of many different nationalities passing out, *20* key in hand, to have a morning glass; and the next moment the fog settled down again upon that part, as brown as umber, and cut him off from his blackguardly surroundings. This was the home of Henry Jekyll's favourite; of a man who was heir to a quarter of a million sterling.

Starting with this extract, explore how Stevenson creates mystery and tension in The Strange Case of Dr. Jekyll and Mr. Hyde.

Write about:

- ***how Stevenson creates mystery and tension in this extract***
- ***how Stevenson creates mystery and tension in the novel as a whole.***

[30 marks] (AO1 = 12; AO2 = 12; AO3 = 6)

(50 Minutes Total = 40 Minutes Writing + 10 Minutes Reading Extract/Making Notes/Planning)

(600 Words Maximum per Essay = 15 Words per Minute)

Stevenson creates a sense of mystery and tension in this extract and his metaphorical description of the "fog" is linked to this theme of mystery, "…here it would be dark like the back-end of evening;" which represents the darkness of the setting and "…in between the swirling wreaths" which conveys the fog as portraying a clear image of death. Throughout the extract there is a contrast between the internal and the external; the hidden and the exposed, "…lamps, which had never been extinguished or had been kindled afresh to combat this mournful re-invasion of darkness," and "...the fog lifted a little" which perhaps points towards the gradual revelation of the mystery of Mr. Hyde.

This disturbing view of the city is linked to Mr. Hyde's personality as it "...seemed, in the lawyer's eyes, like a district of some city in a nightmare." Stevenson writes from the perspective of Utterson, which allows the reader a direct access to his thoughts and feelings. The imagery of the word 'nightmare' and the fact that Mr. Utterson "...was conscious of some touch of that terror" evokes clearly the darkness and the corrosion that he is witnessing. However, this may be influenced by the fact that, "The thoughts of his mind, besides, were of the gloomiest dye;". Stevenson's use of setting and his description of the area "...a dingy street, a gin-palace, ...many ragged children huddled in the doorways," demonstrates the surroundings Hyde has chosen for himself; they are "...blackguardly surroundings." Stevenson further illustrates this theme of darkness through the simile, "...as brown as umber".

Stevenson heightens the sense of mystery and dramatic tension throughout the plot as we witness the gradual unfolding of the mystery of Mr. Hyde. Early in the novella Stevenson states that Utterson holds "...an inordinate, curiosity to behold the features of the real Mr. Hyde" and is convinced that if he could "set eyes on him, ...the mystery would lighten ...as was the habit of mysterious things when well examined." The steady increase of dramatic tension and the sense of mystery that accompanies it is finally resolved at the end of the novella when Utterson is "...to read the two narratives in which this mystery was now to be explained." Stevenson now transitions from the third-person perspective of Mr. Utterson to the first-person perspectives of the letters of Dr. Lanyon and Dr. Jekyll. Stevenson's use of different perspectives thereby allows the characters to directly communicate to the reader and thus establish a rapport.

Stevenson evokes the dark side of life in a city and throughout the novella creates a heightened sense of the fear of the unknown. In Victorian times, definitive ideas as regards class espoused views of a link between poverty and evil and Stevenson's choice of London as his setting suggests that the city was a strange and frightening place for some of its inhabitants. The dark, crowded slums are linked with Hyde's criminality which is in stark contrast to the residences of Dr. Lanyon, Mr. Utterson and Dr. Jekyll. Stevenson also uses the features of the gothic genre, through themes of darkness, neglect and hidden places throughout his novella. This contributes to the increasing and pervasive sense of tension and mystery found throughout his work and in a dramatic context this would have been appreciated during the time he wrote in. Societal expectations are not as clearly defined contemporarily as they were in the Victorian era. However, this perhaps helped Stevenson to present his themes of mystery and tension through his use of contrast in his metaphorical representations of the dualities of Dr. Jekyll and Mr. Hyde.

(600 words)

DR. JEKYLL AND MR. HYDE SIXTH ESSAY – THE RELATIONSHIP BETWEEN MR. UTTERSON AND DR. LANYON

Read the following extract from Chapter 6 and then answer the question that follows.

In this extract, Mr. Utterson visits Dr. Lanyon.

There at least he was not denied admittance; but when he came in, he was shocked at the change which had taken place in the doctor's appearance. He had his death-warrant written legibly upon his face. The rosy man had grown pale; his flesh had fallen away; he was visibly balder and older; and yet it was not so much these tokens of a swift physical decay that arrested the lawyer's notice, as a look in the eye and quality of manner that seemed to testify to some deep-seated terror of the mind. It was unlikely that the doctor should fear death; and yet that was what Utterson was tempted to suspect. "Yes," he thought; "he is a doctor, he must know his own state and that his days are counted; and the knowledge is more than he can bear." And yet when Utterson remarked on his ill-looks, it was with an air of great firmness that Lanyon declared himself a doomed man.

"I have had a shock," he said, "and I shall never recover. It is a question of weeks. Well, life has been pleasant; I liked it; yes, sir, I used to like it. I sometimes think if we knew all, we should be more glad to get away."

"Jekyll is ill, too," observed Utterson. "Have you seen him?"

But Lanyon's face changed, and he held up a trembling hand. "I wish to see or hear no more of Doctor Jekyll," he said in a loud, unsteady voice. "I am quite done with that person; and I beg that you will spare me any allusion to one whom I regard as dead."

"Tut-tut," said Mr. Utterson; and then after a considerable pause, "Can't I do anything?" he inquired. "We are three very old friends, Lanyon; we shall not live to make others."

"Nothing can be done," returned Lanyon; "ask himself."

"He will not see me," said the lawyer.

"I am not surprised at that," was the reply.

"Some day, Utterson, after I am dead, you may perhaps come to learn the right and wrong of this. I cannot tell you. And in the meantime, if you can sit and talk with me of other things, for God's sake, stay and do so; but if you cannot keep clear of this accursed topic, then, in God's name, go, for I cannot bear it."

Starting with this extract, how does Stevenson present the relationship between Mr. Utterson and Dr. Lanyon?

Write about:

• how Stevenson presents their relationship in this extract
• how Stevenson presents the relationship between Mr. Utterson and Dr. Lanyon in the novel as a whole.

[30 marks] (AO1 = 12; AO2 = 12; AO3 = 6)

(50 Minutes Total = 40 Minutes Writing + 10 Minutes Reading Extract/Making Notes/Planning)

(600 Words Maximum per Essay = 15 Words per Minute)

Stevenson presents the relationship between Mr. Utterson and Dr. Lanyon in this extract. Mr. Utterson observes that Dr. Lanyon has "...his death-warrant written legibly upon his face." Stevenson uses a fearful image here and Lanyon appears to also be suffering from a "deep-seated terror of the mind." Lanyon confirms this by proceeding to declare "himself a doomed man" and stating, "'I shall never recover'". The simple sentence, "'It is a question of weeks'" highlights Lanyon's predicament as he states with finality, "'Well, life has been pleasant; I liked it". This highlights both the dramatic development of his physical disintegration and a sudden irreversible change from his former attitudes. However, when Utterson mentions that "'Jekyll is ill, too,'" Lanyon declares with vitriol that he is "...one whom I regard as dead." Lanyon's forceful, hyperbolic phrasing here suggests a strength which is in sharp contrast to his physical state. Stevenson also uses compound sentences and connectives in Lanyon's speech and the meaning of Lanyon's words are ambiguous.

Mr. Utterson appeals to the fact that he, Jekyll and Lanyon "...are three very old friends, and that "'we shall not live to make others.'" Dr. Lanyon, nearing death however, refuses to discuss Jekyll. He appeals to a future time when his friend Utterson may understand the "'right and the wrong of this'" and Stevenson uses both a binary opposite and a clear duality here. It is a sad meeting for Mr. Utterson and Dr. Lanyon as their relationship has been damaged by Lanyon's despair as regards Jekyll's experiments, as Lanyon states, "'I cannot bear it'". Stevenson presents a dramatic and structurally significant moment in this extract and there is a steady increase of dramatic tension beforehand.

This extract is in marked contrast to how Stevenson presents the relationship between Mr. Utterson and Dr. Lanyon in the novella as a whole. When seeking advice as regards Mr. Hyde, Utterson decides that, "'If anyone knows, it will be Lanyon,'". This shows the level of trust and respect he has for Lanyon's insight and counsel. As he arrives at Dr. Lanyon's, "The solemn butler knew and welcomed him;" and "he was subjected to no stage of delay,". Dr. Lanyon's appearance is also diametrically opposed to the extract, as he is a picture of health, "This was a hearty, healthy, dapper, red-faced gentleman,". There is a genuine affection between them as Lanyon, "At sight of Mr.

Utterson, ...sprang up from his chair and welcomed him with both hands." And this greeting "...reposed on genuine feeling." Stevenson states that "...these two were old friends, ... at school and college, both thorough respecters of themselves and of each other" and "men who thoroughly enjoyed each other's company." They are close friends with a warm respect and admiration for one another. Prior to the extract, in a gathering at Dr. Jekyll's home, Stevenson states, "Lanyon had been there; and the face of the host had looked from one to the other as in the old days when the trio were inseparable friends." Mr. Utterson is however, able to gain complete clarity as regards his friends' motivations and actions, when he reads "Doctor Lanyon's Narrative".

Mr. Utterson and Dr. Lanyon are pivotal characters that drive the plot and the dramatic context of this extract would have been appreciated by a Victorian readership. In terms of rules and conformity to societal expectations, Dr. Lanyon's actions may be perceived as ungentlemanly yet religion was important to communities and individuals at this time and Lanyon would reflect the prevalent cautiousness, as regards science and its developments, that existed at the time the novella was written.

(600 words)

By Joseph Anthony Campbell

DR. JEKYLL AND MR. HYDE SEVENTH ESSAY – STEVENSON'S PRESENTATION OF DR. JEKYLL

Read the following extract from Chapter 7 (Incident at the Window) of <u>The Strange Case of Dr. Jekyll and Mr. Hyde</u> and then answer the question that follows.

In this extract, Mr. Utterson and Mr. Enfield are talking to Dr. Jekyll through his window.

The court was very cool and a little damp, and full of premature twilight, although the sky, high up overhead, was still bright with sunset. The middle one of the three windows was half-way open; and sitting close beside it, taking the air with an infinite sadness of
5 mien, like some disconsolate prisoner, Utterson saw Dr. Jekyll.
"What! Jekyll!" he cried. "I trust you are better."
"I am very low, Utterson," replied the doctor drearily, "very low. It will not last long, thank God."
"You stay too much indoors," said the lawyer. "You should be out,
10 whipping up the circulation like Mr. Enfield and me. (This is my cousin—Mr. Enfield—Dr. Jekyll.) Come now; get your hat and take a quick turn with us."
"You are very good," sighed the other. "I should like to very much;

but no, no, no, it is quite impossible; I dare not. But indeed, Utterson,
15 I am very glad to see you; this is really a great pleasure; I would ask you and Mr. Enfield up, but the place is really not fit."
"Why then," said the lawyer good-naturedly, "the best thing we can do is to stay down here and speak with you from where we are."
"That is just what I was about to venture to propose," returned the
20 doctor, with a smile. But the words were hardly uttered, before the smile was struck out of his face and succeeded by an expression of such abject terror and despair as froze the very blood of the two gentlemen below. They saw it but for a glimpse, for the window was instantly thrust down; but that glimpse had been sufficient, and they
25 turned and left the court without a word.

Starting with this extract, how does Stevenson present Dr. Jekyll?

Write about:

• *how Stevenson presents Dr. Jekyll in this extract*
• *how Stevenson presents Dr. Jekyll in the novel as a whole.*

[30 marks] (AO1 = 12; AO2 = 12; AO3 = 6)

(50 Minutes Total = 40 Minutes Writing + 10 Minutes Reading Extract/Making Notes/Planning)

(600 Words Maximum per Essay = 15 Words per Minute)

Stevenson presents Dr. Jekyll in this extract as a "disconsolate prisoner" in his own home, "...taking the air with an infinite sadness of mien,". The simile, "like a disconsolate prisoner" is in fact a reality now for Jekyll, who is attempting to cage his alter-ego Hyde. Stevenson's use of language, such as, "infinite sadness", emphasises Jekyll's suffering. Stevenson's description that the "court" is "full of premature twilight," also conveys a dark sense of the atmosphere and possibly symbolises Jekyll's mood.

Dr. Jekyll experiences temporary relief through conversing with Utterson in this extract when Stevenson suddenly describes an abrupt change in Jekyll's behaviour, "…the smile was struck out of his face and succeeded by an expression of such abject terror and despair as froze the very blood of the two gentlemen below." Stevenson's use of the word 'struck' perhaps conveys the violence of the sudden appearance of Mr. Hyde, as if Hyde is attacking Jekyll from within, which changes Jekyll's behaviour instantly. The words 'terror' and 'despair' demonstrate that Jekyll has lost all control of when the transformations will now occur. In terms of conformity to societal expectations, Jekyll's window being "instantly thrust down" would have been perceived as ungentlemanly in the Victorian era, yet it is Jekyll's expression that "froze the very blood of the two gentlemen below". Stevenson uses a fearful, metaphorical image here, to demonstrate the violence of Jekyll's transformation that can even be experienced somewhat viscerally by those observing it.

Stevenson presents Dr. Jekyll (and Mr. Hyde) as the central character of the novella. Jekyll is a loyal friend, kind master and a man with an amiable disposition. He is well-respected, wealthy, intelligent and ambitious. His intelligence is clearly delineated by Stevenson with the line "Henry Jekyll, M.D., D.C.L., LL.D., F.R.S" and he is described as a "…large, well-made, smooth-faced man of fifty with something of a slyish cast". In this description, Stevenson's use of term, 'slyish cast' points towards a deceitful nature within Jekyll.

Jekyll's statement at the end of the novella is presented through a first-person perspective by Stevenson, which allows the character to directly communicate to the reader and thus establish a rapport. This allows the reader to perhaps have some sympathy with Jekyll as he begins his experiment with good intentions and journeys towards his own personal hell and ultimate destruction. His experiment causes him to become erratic and alienated from his friends and Victorian society. Jekyll continually attempts to conceal Mr. Hyde's true identity and to control the uncontrollable transformations that result from his experiment. He becomes unpredictable as he attempts to resist the addictive hold of Hyde but ultimately, he and Hyde each lose their struggle to become the dominant personality and perish. Dr. Jekyll is finally discovered as the transformed Mr. Hyde with a "crushed phial in the hand", a metaphor for how the very science that Dr. Jekyll loved, destroys him. He is described by Stevenson as a "self-destroyer" - which in the Victorian era would have been considered a sin; an unnatural end to the natural course of one's life.

In terms of the social and historical context of the novel, it takes place in the Victorian era after the 'Industrial Revolution'. The shift from a more 'natural' way of living to a technological and scientific way is reflected in Jekyll's experiment - as he changes the natural course of his being through science. Stevenson presents Dr. Jekyll as a gothic hero who goes beyond the boundaries of Victorian morality and its restrictions through an addictive need to realise his experiment which ultimately results in his untimely destruction.

(600 words)

DR. JEKYLL AND MR. HYDE EIGHTH ESSAY – MR. HYDE AS INHUMAN AND DISTURBING

Read the following extract from Chapter 8 (The Last Night) of <u>The Strange Case of Dr. Jekyll and Mr. Hyde</u> and then answer the question that follows.

In this extract Poole, Jekyll's servant, talks with Utterson about events at Jekyll's house.

"That's it!" said Poole. "It was this way. I came suddenly into the theatre from the garden. It seems he had slipped out to look for this drug, or whatever it is; for the cabinet door was open, and there he was at the far end of the room digging among the crates. He looked up when I came in, gave a kind of cry, and whipped
5 upstairs into the cabinet. It was but for one minute that I saw him, but the hair stood up on my head like quills. Sir, if that was my master, why had he a mask upon his face? If it was my master, why did he cry out like a rat, and run from me? I have served him long enough. And then …", the man paused and passed his hand over his face.
10 "These are all very strange circumstances," said Mr. Utterson, "but I think I begin to see daylight. Your master, Poole, is plainly seized with one of those maladies that both torture and deform the sufferer; hence, for aught I know, the alteration of his voice; hence the mask and his avoidance of his friends; hence his

eagerness to find this drug, by means of which the poor soul retains some hope
15 of ultimate recovery – God grant that he be not deceived. There is my explanation; it is sad enough, Poole, ay, and appalling to consider; but it is plain and natural, hangs well together, and delivers us from all exorbitant alarms."
"Sir," said the butler, turning to a sort of mottled pallor, "that thing was not my master, and there's the truth. My master" – here he looked round him and began
20 to whisper – "is a tall, fine build of a man, and this was more of a dwarf." Utterson attempted to protest. "O sir," cried Poole, "do you think I do not know my master after twenty years? do you think I do not know where his head comes to in the cabinet door, where I saw him every morning of my life? No, sir, that thing in the mask was never Dr. Jekyll – God knows what it was, but it was never Dr. Jekyll;
25 and it is the belief of my heart that there was murder done."

Starting with this extract, explore how Stevenson presents Mr Hyde as an inhuman and disturbing member of society.

Write about:

• *how Stevenson presents Mr Hyde in this extract*
• *how Stevenson presents Mr Hyde as an inhuman and disturbing member of society in the novel as a whole.*

[30 marks] (AO1 = 12; AO2 = 12; AO3 = 6)

(50 Minutes Total = 40 Minutes Writing + 10 Minutes Reading Extract/Making Notes/Planning)

(600 Words Maximum per Essay = 15 Words per Minute)

Stevenson presents Mr. Hyde in this extract as Poole relates Hyde's strange and secretive behaviour, "'He looked up when I came in, gave a kind of cry, and whipped upstairs into the cabinet.'" This has a shocking impact on Poole as he states, "'…the hair stood up on my head". Throughout the extract, Poole is clearly physically shaken and paranoid as he relates his words to Utterson, "…paused and passed his hand over his face", his skin "…turning to a sort of mottled pallor," and "…looked round him and began to whisper". Poole declares to Utterson, "'…why had he a mask upon his face?'" and this use of the imagery of a 'mask' highlights the theme of secrecy that is present throughout the novella. Stevenson also uses animal imagery as Poole asks "'…why did he cry out like a rat, and run from me?'" and Poole continues his use of questions, stating to Utterson: "'…do you think I do not know my master after twenty years?'" He mentions the contrast in their height also, as Jekyll "…is a tall, fine build of a man, and this was more of a dwarf." Hyde's stature as a 'dwarf' and the use of the word "thing" to refer to Hyde by Poole "'…that thing in the mask was never Dr. Jekyll", demonstrates the strength of Poole's conviction that his master was a different man. This is demonstrated through Stevenson's use of fearful, animalistic imagery and through Poole's forceful, hyperbolic phrasing in this extract. The effect of Hyde's inhumanity and his disturbing qualities are clearly reflected through Poole's reactions as he describes him.

Stevenson presents Mr. Hyde in the novella as a whole as a mysterious criminal who has a great propensity for violence. He commits horrific acts and shows no repentance nor accepts any responsibility for his actions. As readers, we are first aware of Hyde's behaviour when he tramples upon an innocent young girl, i.e., "'…trampled calmly over the child's body and left her screaming on the ground.". This is a shocking image and conveys a disturbing lack of morality in Hyde's behaviour. He becomes increasingly more violent and commits further terrible and heinous acts - culminating in the murder of Danvers Carew, which has a shocking resonance to the incident with the young girl as, "…with ape-like fury, he was trampling his victim under foot,". Again, Stevenson describes Hyde in animalistic terms and Hyde lacks any sense of humanity here. Stevenson states that people's view of Hyde and upon which they all "…agreed…was the haunting sense of unexpressed deformity with which the fugitive impressed his beholders." The use of the word 'haunting' by Stevenson further illustrates Hyde's inhuman and disturbing nature.

Hyde's violent acts represent his selfish, primitive urges and in the context of the times, this would have been abhorrent to Victorian religious morality. Hyde's lack of conscience would also have shocked the Victorian readers of the time due to their religious beliefs. However, in terms of dramatic context, the spectacle of Mr. Hyde's actions would have been appreciated by Victorian readers as Mr. Hyde is a key element of the literary gothic genre that Stevenson writes in, which describes the sinister, the grotesque and the mysterious. Mr. Hyde is a dark and doomed character and a literary character is never entirely separate from the author and Stevenson himself may have struggled with the rules and conformity of the societal expectations of the time. However, Hyde's murderous and cruel nature is presented by Stevenson overall as being both disturbing and inhuman and as displaying a complete disregard for society's conventions.

(600 words)

By Joseph Anthony Campbell

DR. JEKYLL AND MR. HYDE NINTH ESSAY – THE RELATIONSHIP BETWEEN MR. HYDE/DR. JEKYLL AND DR. LANYON

Read the following extract from Chapter 9 and then answer the question that follows.

In this extract Dr. Lanyon describes a discussion with Mr. Hyde (Dr. Jekyll).

He sprang to it, and then paused, and laid his hand upon his heart; I could hear his teeth grate with the convulsive action of his jaws; and his face was so ghastly to see that I grew alarmed both for his life and reason.
"Compose yourself," said I.
He turned a dreadful smile to me, and as if with the decision of despair, plucked away the sheet. At sight of the contents, he uttered one loud sob of such immense relief that I sat petrified. And the next moment, in a voice that was already fairly well under control, "Have you a graduated glass?" he asked.
I rose from my place with something of an effort and gave him what he asked.

He thanked me with a smiling nod, measured out a few minims of the red tincture and added one of the powders. The mixture, which was at first of a reddish hue, began, in proportion as the crystals melted, to brighten in colour, to effervesce audibly, and to throw off small fumes of vapour. Suddenly and at the same moment, the ebullition ceased and the compound changed to a dark purple, which faded again more slowly to a watery green. My visitor, who had watched these metamorphoses with a keen eye, smiled, set down the glass upon the table, and then turned and looked upon me with an air of scrutiny.

"And now," said he, "to settle what remains. Will you be wise? will you be guided? will you suffer me to take this glass in my hand and to go forth from your house without further parley? or has the greed of curiosity too much command of you? Think before you answer, for it shall be done as you decide. As you decide, you shall be left as you were before, and neither richer nor wiser, unless the sense of service rendered to a man in mortal distress may be counted as a kind of riches of the soul. Or, if you shall so prefer to choose, a new province of knowledge and new avenues to fame and power shall be laid open to you, here, in this room, upon the instant; and your sight shall be blasted by a prodigy to stagger the unbelief of Satan."

Starting with this extract, how does Stevenson present the relationship between Mr. Hyde/Dr. Jekyll and Dr. Lanyon?

Write about:

• *how Stevenson presents the relationship between Mr. Hyde/Dr. Jekyll and Dr. Lanyon in this extract*
• *how Stevenson presents the relationship between Mr. Hyde/Dr. Jekyll and Dr. Lanyon in the novel as a whole.*

[30 marks] (AO1 = 12; AO2 = 12; AO3 = 6)

(50 Minutes Total = 40 Minutes Writing + 10 Minutes Reading Extract/Making Notes/Planning)

(600 Words Maximum per Essay = 15 Words per Minute)

Stevenson presents the relationship between Dr. Jekyll (who is transformed into his alter-ego Mr. Hyde) and Dr. Lanyon in this extract. There is a build-up of dramatic tension prior to this extract as Lanyon has retrieved the contents of a cabinet in Dr. Jekyll's laboratory and he has agreed to meet Dr. Jekyll's 'messenger' at midnight.

Lanyon states of Hyde that, "I could hear his teeth grate with the convulsive action of his jaws;". This is a fearful image and the fact that Mr. Hyde's 'teeth grate' heightens Stevenson's presentation of Hyde's animalistic behaviour as he is anxious, frustrated and eager to devour something. Lanyon also states of Hyde, "...his face was so ghastly to see that I grew alarmed". The word 'ghastly' demonstrates the horrific and terrifying nature of Hyde's appearance and the fact that Lanyon 'grew alarmed' demonstrates his fear. The dramatic nature of this moment reflects its significance within the novella as a whole.

In Lanyon's presence, Hyde mixes his potion. He then offers Lanyon a choice as to whether he is to observe what is to follow, "'Will you be wise? ...or has the greed of curiosity too much command of you?'" Lanyon could remove himself from the 'ghastly' presence of Hyde and receive as Hyde states a "'...kind of riches of the soul'" for helping him, or remain. It is to be a life-or-death decision for Lanyon and as Lanyon remains, Hyde states, "'...your sight shall be blasted by a prodigy'". Hyde's forceful, hyperbolic phrasing here suggests strength as he is soon to reveal the subtext behind his words.

Stevenson presents the relationship between Dr. Jekyll (Mr. Hyde) and Dr. Lanyon throughout the novella. Dr. Hastie Lanyon, a long-time friend of Jekyll, fundamentally disagrees with Jekyll's concepts of science, describing them as "'...too fanciful'" and "'unscientific balderdash.'" Early in the novella, when Utterson states "'you and I must be the two oldest friends that Henry Jekyll has?'", Jekyll is again a source of tension for Lanyon as he replies, "'I see little of him now.'". When Utterson probes further and asks "'I thought you had a bond of common interest.'" Lanyon replies briefly, "'We had,'". A chasm has grown between Dr. Jekyll and Dr. Lanyon over a period of "'more than ten years'". Dr. Jekyll also states, "'I was never more disappointed in any man than Lanyon.'" Yet, shortly before the extract there appears to be a restoration of former affections as when Dr. Jekyll hosts a dinner party, Stevenson states, "...the face of the host had looked from one to the other as in the old days when the trio were inseparable friends." Yet, in the form of Mr. Hyde, Dr. Jekyll reveals his anger towards Lanyon, "'...you who have derided your superiors—behold!". Lanyon also mentions "'God'" throughout the novella and his more natural way of being, places him in juxtaposition to Jekyll, who is relentless in his goal of releasing his hidden self, i.e., Mr. Hyde. He will brook no opposition to this, (including Dr. Lanyon's) and thus Dr. Jekyll binds himself to unnatural and even supernatural forces.

In the Victorian era, religion was important to communities and individuals. Consequently, people were cautious and superstitious of science and its developments. Stevenson's descriptions of the sinister, the grotesque and the mysterious are key elements of the gothic genre, and the contrast of the 'natural' science of Dr. Lanyon and the dark, unnatural acts of Dr. Jekyll and his alter ego Mr. Hyde, serve as an intertwining metaphor. The dramatic context and spectacle of Stevenson's novella would have been greatly appreciated during his time.

(600 words)

By Joseph Anthony Campbell

DR. JEKYLL AND MR. HYDE TENTH ESSAY – DR. LANYON

Read the following extract from Chapter 9 and then answer the question that follows.

In this extract Dr. Lanyon recalls a meeting with Mr. Hyde.

"Sir," said I, affecting a coolness that I was far from truly possessing, "you speak enigmas, and you will perhaps not wonder that I hear you with no very strong impression of belief. But I have gone too far in the way of inexplicable services to pause before I see the end."
"It is well," replied my visitor. "Lanyon, you remember your vows: what follows is under the seal of our profession. And now, you who have so long been bound to the most narrow and material views, you who have denied the virtue of transcendental medicine, you who have derided your superiors—behold!"
He put the glass to his lips and drank at one gulp. A cry followed; he reeled, staggered, clutched at the table and held on, staring with injected eyes, gasping with open mouth; and as I looked there came, I thought, a change—he seemed to swell—his face became suddenly black and the features seemed to melt and alter—and the next moment, I had sprung to my feet and leaped back against the wall, my arm raised to shield me from that prodigy, my mind submerged in terror.
"O God!" I screamed, and "O God!" again and again; for there before my eyes—pale and shaken and half fainting, and groping before him with his hands, like a man restored from death—there stood Henry Jekyll!

What he told me in the next hour, I cannot bring my mind to set on paper. I saw what I saw, I heard what I heard, and my soul sickened at it; and yet now when that sight has faded from my eyes, I ask myself if I believe it, and I cannot answer. My life is shaken to its roots; sleep has left me; the deadliest terror sits by me at all hours of the day and night; I feel that my days are numbered, and that I must die; and yet I shall die incredulous.

Starting with this extract, how does Stevenson present Dr. Lanyon?

Write about:

• *how Stevenson presents Dr. Lanyon in this extract*
• *how Stevenson presents Dr. Lanyon in the novel as a whole.*

[30 marks] (AO1 = 12; AO2 = 12; AO3 = 6)

(50 Minutes Total = 40 Minutes Writing + 10 Minutes Reading Extract/Making Notes/Planning)

(600 Words Maximum per Essay = 15 Words per Minute)

Stevenson presents Dr. Lanyon witnessing Hyde's transformation into Dr. Jekyll, in this extract. Hyde warns Lanyon, "'remember…the seal of our profession'" and thus reveals that he is a fellow scientist before angrily and arrogantly declaring to Lanyon, "'And now, …you who have denied the virtue of transcendental medicine'". The forceful, hyperbolic phrasing here suggests a sense of grandiosity which is in stark contrast to Lanyon who appeals to God, "O God!" I screamed, and "O God!" again and again;". The precision of speech here suggests that Dr. Lanyon is almost speechless and he is also deeply affected both physically and mentally; "…my arm raised to shield me from that prodigy, my mind submerged in terror."

After witnessing the transformation, Lanyon despondently states, "I saw what I saw, I heard what I heard, and my soul sickened at it; … I ask myself if I believe it, and I cannot answer. My life is shaken to its roots;". Lanyon uses fearful, metaphorical images here and Stevenson gives us a glimpse into Dr. Lanyon's state of mind. Stevenson repeats the word 'I' here seven times in this quotation to reinforce Dr. Lanyon's incredulity ("I shall die incredulous"), as he cannot believe what he has witnessed and doubts the very existence of what he has witnessed. Dr. Lanyon's deepest sense of self is negatively impacted by Dr. Jekyll's experiment, "'…the deadliest terror sits by me at all hours of the day and night;". It is both a dramatic and structurally significant moment in the novella.

Stevenson presents Dr. Lanyon in the novella as a whole as a pivotal character that drives the plot. Stevenson states of Dr. Lanyon, Dr. Jekyll and Mr. Utterson that "…the trio were inseparable friends". However, when Utterson mentions Jekyll to Lanyon, (after Lanyon has been deeply scarred by Jekyll's unnatural transformation) he replies, "I wish to see or hear no more of Doctor Jekyll …I am quite done with that person; and I beg that you will spare me any allusion to one whom I regard as dead.". Stevenson presents Lanyon's emotions clearly here – he was once one of Jekyll's oldest friends yet now views him as 'dead'. The repetition of 'I' by Stevenson again illustrates that the language Lanyon uses is charged with personal passion and emotion.

Following the visit of Mr. Utterson, "A week afterwards Dr. Lanyon took to his bed, and in something less than a fortnight he is dead." The short, sudden and shocking time period presented here illustrates the rapidity of Dr. Lanyon's deterioration due to Dr. Jekyll's revelation. However, before his death, Lanyon gives Utterson, his close personal friend, a letter to be opened after Jekyll's death or disappearance. Dr. Lanyon is the first person to discover Hyde's true identity and to subsequently hear Jekyll's private confession. In 'Doctor Lanyon's Narrative' Lanyon describes the actions of Jekyll and his thoughts and reactions to the transformation.

Dr. Lanyon's horrified response to Jekyll's transformation would represent the natural response that would have been implicit within the Victorian morality of the time. This is in stark contrast to Jekyll's unnatural and immoral experiment and his creation Mr.

Hyde; who is presented in Stevenson's gothic novel as sinister and grotesque. This contrast of Dr. Lanyon and the dark acts of Dr. Jekyll and Mr. Hyde, therefore serve as a metaphor between good and evil at a time when religion was vitally important to communities and individuals and when people were increasingly wary of science and its rapid developments. The dramatic context and spectacle of this novella would have therefore been greatly enjoyed by contemporary readers.

(600 words)

DR. JEKYLL AND MR. HYDE ELEVENTH ESSAY – STEVENSON'S PRESENTATION OF DR. JEKYLL AS CONFLICTED

Read the following extract from Chapter 10 (Henry Jekyll's Full Statement of the Case) of <u>The Strange Case of Dr. Jekyll and Mr. Hyde</u> and then answer the question that follows.

In this extract, Jekyll reflects upon his life.

I was born in the year 18— to a large fortune, endowed besides with excellent parts, inclined by nature to industry, fond of the respect of the wise and good among my fellow-men, and thus, as might have been supposed, with every guarantee of an honourable and distinguished future. And indeed the worst of my faults was a certain impatient gaiety of disposition, such as has made the happiness of many, but such as I found it hard to reconcile with my imperious desire to carry my head high, and wear a more than commonly grave countenance before the public. Hence it came about that I concealed my pleasures; and that when I reached years of reflection, and began to look round me and take stock of my progress and position in the world, I stood already committed to a profound duplicity of life. Many a man would have even blazoned such irregularities as I was guilty of; but from the high views that I had set before me, I regarded and hid them with an almost morbid sense of shame. It was thus rather the exacting nature of my aspirations than any particular degradation in my faults, that made me what I was and, with even a deeper trench than in the majority of men, severed in me those provinces of good and ill which divide and compound man's dual nature. In this case, I was driven to reflect deeply and inveterately on that hard law of life, which lies at the root of religion and is one of the most plentiful springs of distress. Though so profound a double-dealer, I was in no sense a hypocrite; both sides of me were in dead earnest; I was no more myself when I laid aside restraint and plunged in shame, than when I laboured, in the eye of day, at the furtherance of knowledge or the relief of sorrow and suffering. And it chanced that the direction of my scientific studies, which led wholly towards the mystic and the transcendental, reacted and shed a strong light on this consciousness of the perennial war among my members. With every day, and from both sides of my intelligence, the moral and the intellectual, I thus drew steadily nearer to that truth, by whose partial discovery I have been doomed to such a dreadful shipwreck: that man is not truly one, but truly two.

Starting with this extract, how does Stevenson present Dr. Jekyll as a conflicted character?

Write about:

• how Stevenson presents Dr. Jekyll as conflicted in this extract
• how Stevenson presents Dr. Jekyll as conflicted in the novel as a whole.

[30 marks] (AO1 = 12; AO2 = 12; AO3 = 6)

(50 Minutes Total = 40 Minutes Writing + 10 Minutes Reading Extract/Making Notes/Planning)

(600 Words Maximum per Essay = 15 Words per Minute)

Stevenson presents Dr. Jekyll as conflicted in this extract as exemplified by Jekyll's statement that, "I stood already committed to a profound duplicity of life." The theme of Jekyll being a conflicted character is accentuated by the fact that he experiences a "perennial war among my members." Stevenson's novella can be interpreted as an examination of the duality of human nature as Dr. Jekyll battles between the benevolence and malevolence within himself, that he feels are not fitting for a man of his stature, "Hence it came about that I concealed my pleasures;". Therefore, as Jekyll indulges in his vices, he feels "an almost morbid sense of shame."

Stevenson uses the first-person narrative of Dr. Jekyll in this extract. This gives the reader direct access to the character's thoughts and feelings and thus establishes a rapport. The confessional nature of Jekyll's statement may endear him to readers as he explains that the experiment he created was due in part to, "the exacting nature of my aspirations than any particular degradation in my faults,". Stevenson presents Dr. Jekyll as a well-respected, intelligent and wealthy scientist born with "every guarantee of an honourable and distinguished future". Yet, the fact that he was "led wholly towards the mystic and the transcendental" and to meld the binary opposites of the natural and the supernatural, leads him to the state of being, "doomed to such a dreadful shipwreck:". Yet as a refrain, Jekyll (and therefore perhaps Stevenson) states with emphasis, "that man is not truly one, but truly two" thus claiming that a conflicting duality exists within all people.

Stevenson presents Dr. Jekyll as conflicted in the novella as a whole and as an effective and pivotal character that drives the plot. Jekyll develops a potion to effectively mask his darker side and thus creates Mr. Hyde, in order to relieve the conflict within himself. However, ironically, he becomes entirely conflicted and barely able to maintain a semblance of himself as Hyde strives for domination and possession of Jekyll's physical form, "It took on this occasion a double dose to recall me to myself; and alas!". Eventually, his ability to change from Hyde and to regain himself is lost. As he composes his final letter, he is aware that this conflict will soon be at an end and that he will become Hyde permanently. Earlier in the novella he states, "It will not last long, thank God" and at the end of his letter he states, "I bring the life of that unhappy Henry Jekyll to an end." and thus he brings his statement and the novella to a close. It appears however that Jekyll and Hyde are in conflict, even in death, as, "there lay the body of a man sorely contorted and still twitching." and "the cords of his face moved with a semblance of life, but life was quite gone;". The 'twitching' and the moving are like aftershocks of a conflict that is now brought to an end and resolved by Stevenson.

The duplicity of human nature is presented by Stevenson in Dr. Jekyll and Mr. Hyde and it is a pervasive theme throughout the novella. The Victorian concern of having outward respectability is also presented, as there is a central duality and conflict between Jekyll's inner, forbidden desires and the mask of social respectability that he wears. The religious nature of Victorian society promoted the suppression of forbidden desires and Stevenson himself, may have experienced this sense of duality, as a dramatic character such as Dr. Jekyll is not a human being with mental processes separate from those of the author.

(600 words)

By Joseph Anthony Campbell

DR. JEKYLL AND MR. HYDE TWELFTH ESSAY – THE THEMES OF GOOD AND EVIL

Read the following extract from Chapter 10 (Henry Jekyll's Full Statement of the Case) of <u>The Strange Case of Dr. Jekyll and Mr. Hyde</u> *and then answer the question that follows.*

In this extract, Jekyll describes his experience of taking the potion for the first time.

I knew myself, at the first breath of this new life, to be more wicked, tenfold more wicked, sold a slave to my original evil; and the thought, in that moment, braced and delighted me like wine. I stretched out my hands, exulting in the freshness of these sensations; and in the act I was suddenly aware that I had
5 lost in stature.
There was no mirror, at that date, in my room; that which stands beside me as I write was brought there later on, and for the very purpose of these transformations. The night, however, was far gone into the morning – the morning, black as it was, was nearly ripe for the conception of the day – the
10 inmates of my house were locked in the most rigorous hours of slumber; and I determined, flushed as I was with hope and triumph, to venture in my new shape as far as to my bedroom. I crossed the yard, wherein the constellations looked down upon me, I could have thought, with wonder, the first creature of that sort

that their unsleeping vigilance had yet disclosed to them; I stole through the
15 corridors, a stranger in my own house; and, coming to my room, I saw for the first
time the appearance of Edward Hyde.

I must here speak by theory alone, saying not that which I know, but that
which I suppose to be most probable. The evil side of my nature, to which I had
now transferred the stamping efficacy, was less robust and less developed than
20 the good which I had just deposed. Again, in the course of my life, which had
been, after all, nine-tenths a life of effort, virtue, and control, it had been much
less exercised and much less exhausted. And hence, as I think, it came about
that Edward Hyde was so much smaller, slighter, and younger than Henry Jekyll.
Even as good shone upon the countenance of the one, evil was written broadly
25 and plainly on the face of the other. Evil besides (which I must still believe to be
the lethal side of man) had left on that body an imprint of deformity and decay.
And yet when I looked upon that ugly idol in the glass, I was conscious of no
repugnance, rather of a leap of welcome. This too, was myself. It seemed
natural and human. In my eyes it bore a livelier image of the spirit, it seemed
30 more express and single, than the imperfect and divided countenance I had been
hitherto accustomed to call mine. And in so far I was doubtless right. I have
observed that when I bore the semblance of Edward Hyde, none could come
near to me at first without a visible misgiving of the flesh. This, as I take it, was
because all human beings, as we meet them, are commingled out of good and
35 evil: and Edward Hyde, alone in the ranks of mankind, was pure evil.

Starting with this extract, explore how Stevenson presents ideas about good and evil in *The Strange Case of Dr. Jekyll and Mr. Hyde*.

Write about:

• *how Stevenson presents ideas about good and evil in this extract*
• *how Stevenson presents ideas about good and evil in the novel as a whole.*

[30 marks] (AO1 = 12; AO2 = 12; AO3 = 6)

(50 Minutes Total = 40 Minutes Writing + 10 Minutes Reading Extract/Making Notes/Planning)

(600 Words Maximum per Essay = 15 Words per Minute)

Stevenson presents ideas about good and evil in this extract such as the temptation and attraction of evil for Dr. Jekyll, who after his transformation states that he was "flushed …with hope and triumph," as he experienced the "freshness of these sensations;". However, there is a tension here as he is "sold a slave to my original evil;" and he was "a stranger in my own house;" and refers to Hyde as "the first creature of that sort". The word 'creature' points to the reality of Hyde being a manifestation of evil.

Jekyll, as a reputable member of society theorises that "The evil side of my nature," was "less developed than the good which I had just deposed." Stevenson uses imagery associated with pain and sickness to Hyde, "Evil besides …had left on that body an imprint of deformity and decay" and refers explicitly to Jekyll's loss of stature "Edward Hyde was so much smaller, slighter, …than Henry Jekyll." Indeed, Hyde's very nature is so repulsive that "none could come near to me at first without a visible misgiving of the flesh." Stevenson refers directly to both good and evil when he states of Jekyll that "Even as good shone upon the countenance of the one" that "Edward Hyde, alone in the ranks of mankind, was pure evil." Mr. Hyde is separate from "all human beings, …commingled out of good and evil", in that he is the only 'creature' to lack duality in his nature which is a fearful and terrifying image. Stevenson also repeats the word 'evil' throughout this extract to reinforce the dramatic significance of this initial transformation of Dr. Jekyll into the 'pure evil' of Mr. Hyde.

Stevenson presents ideas about good and evil in the novella as a whole as he writes about the duality of human nature and the idea that every single human being is capable of good and evil deeds. Dr. Jekyll is a man who has repressed evil within and he seeks his own twisted pleasures through Mr. Hyde in an attempt to mask this hidden evil. Freud believed that banishing 'evil' to the unconscious mind in an attempt to achieve perfect goodness could result in the development of a Mr. Hyde-type manifestation in one's conscious behaviour. Hyde could therefore be the physical and mental manifestation of Jekyll's latent 'evil' personality.

Stevenson was intrigued by the idea of how human personalities reflect the interplay of good and evil i.e., "Jekyll was no worse; he woke again to his good qualities seemingly unimpaired;" and how once again he would attempt to redeem himself, "he would even make haste, …to undo the evil done by Hyde." As Jekyll indulges hubristically, "comparing myself with other men, …with the lazy cruelty of their neglect", he finds himself transformed once again into Hyde. It is evident that even without Hyde, Jekyll has "those provinces of good and ill which divide and compound man's dual nature."

In terms of the social and historical context, Victorian society held heavily entrenched views and attitudes as regards the importance of respectability and reputation. The pious nature of Victorian society therefore meant that many people suppressed their desires and feelings in order to avoid experiencing shame. In the Victorian era, many people were religious and believed in satanic influence when people committed evil acts and crimes. Many texts from the Victorian period shared this motif. Stevenson's novella presents a clear theme of the opposition of good and evil within people. Modern readers, however, are less inclined towards a belief in the binary opposites of good and evil than Stevenson's contemporary Victorian readers.

(600 words)

ASSESSMENT OBJECTIVES

There are **four assessment objectives** assessed in each English Literature examination: (**no A04 assessment for this section**) AO1, (12 Marks) AO2 (12 Marks) AO3 (6 Marks) and AO4 (4 marks for Spelling and Grammar).

AO1 = Read, understand and respond to the text ('**The Strange Case of Dr. Jekyll and Mr. Hyde'**) and the task set in the question. Use 4 to 6 quotations you may have memorised from the novella (or memorise those that I have provided in my answers in this book on various characters/themes in the novella).

AO2 = Analyse the language, form and structure used by a writer (**Stevenson**) to create meanings and effects i.e., also mention '**Stevenson**' 4 to 6 times or more in your answer and how he presents characters/themes and creates meanings and effects.

AO3 = is the understanding of the relationship between the ideas in the text and the context/time in which the text was written and the context within which the text is set.

AO4 = spell and punctuate with consistent accuracy, and consistently use vocabulary and sentence structures to achieve control of the meaning you are aiming to convey.

The Assessment Objectives are not provided in the examination itself. However, I have provided which assessment objectives are being assessed in the practice questions in this book. It is important to be aware of the structure of how the assessment objectives are allocated in each question of the exam in order to maximise your opportunities to obtain full marks in each question.

It is a good idea also to plan your answer before you begin writing it. A plan will mean you answer the question in an organised and sequenced manner. Your newfound understanding of the assessment objectives will also ensure you have met all of the required criteria.

TIMINGS

Please allocate the correct words per minute per mark! Again, to re-iterate: The best approach is to spend 50 minutes on each question - 40 minutes writing and 10 minutes making notes, planning and checking your final answer for basic corrections at the end of the examination.

If you have extra time allocated to you, just change the calculation to accommodate the extra time you have i.e., if you have 25% extra time (= 50 minutes writing per question = 12 words per minute and 20 words per mark) and if you have 50% extra time (= 1 hour writing per question = 10 words per minute and 20 words per mark) also equals a 600-word essay for each section. Please **move on from the set question as soon as you have reached or are coming towards your time limit**. This ensures that you have excellent coverage of your whole exam and therefore attain a very good mark.

Similar to all the principles in this book, **you must apply and follow the correct timings for each question and stick to them throughout your exam to get an A star (Grade 9) in your English Literature examinations.** Without applying this principle in these examinations (and to a large extent all examinations) you cannot achieve the highest marks! **Apply all of the principles provided in this book to succeed!**

APPROXIMATE WORD COUNT PER QUESTION

Now that you know what is on each examination, how the assessment objectives are assessed and the time allocated for each type of question; we come to what would be considered the correct word count per mark for each question. *The primary principle though is to spend the right amount of time on each question.*

In the answers in this book, I have provided the maximum word count theoretically possible for each answer which works out at **15 words per minute and 20 words per mark and therefore this equals a 600-word essay for each section on Paper 1**. If your answer has quality, this gives you the very best chance of obtaining the highest marks in your English Literature exam. Obviously, it does not if you are waffling however. (Please remember to answer the question set and to move on in the time allocated.)

I am aware that some students can write faster than others but all should be able to write 10 words per minute and thus a 400-word essay in the time (if they have not been allocated extra time). This is where conciseness is important in your writing.

My students and readers have applied all of the techniques of the Quality Control System™ I am providing you with; to gain A stars (Grade 9's) in their examinations. You can replicate them by following the advice in this book.

Thank you for purchasing this book and best wishes for your examinations!
Joseph

AUTHOR'S NOTE

This book will provide you with 12 crystal clear and accurate examples of 'A' star grade (Grade 9) AQA GCSE English Literature **'The Strange Case of Dr. Jekyll and Mr. Hyde'** answers from the **'19th - century novel'** section of the new syllabus and enables students to achieve the same grade in their upcoming examinations.

I teach both GCSE and A level English and Psychology and I am a qualified and experienced teacher and tutor of over 20 years standing. I teach, write and provide independent tuition in central and west London.

The resources in this book WILL help you to get an A star (Grade 9) in your GCSE English Literature examinations, as they have done and will continue to do so, for my students.

Best wishes,

Joseph

ABOUT THE AUTHOR

I graduated from the Universities of Liverpool and Leeds and I obtained first class honours in my teacher training.

I have taught and provided private tuition for over 20 years up to university level. I also write academic resources for the Times Educational Supplement.

My tuition students, (and now, my thousands of readers), have been fortunate enough to attain places to study at Oxford, Cambridge and Imperial College, London and other Russell Group Universities. The students have done very well in their examinations. I hope and know that my English Literature books can enable you to take the next step on your academic journey.

LIMITED AVAILABILITY FOR ONLINE AND IN PERSON (IN LONDON) GCSE ENGLISH TUITION WITH ME.

Thank you again, for purchasing my book. I want you to be the first to know that I currently have some limited availability for GCSE English tuition. I am able to tutor in person, in London, or online.

Click or type the link/s below into your search engine to begin your journey of having one on one proven, expert tuition with me; in order to ensure that you reach the highest levels that you are fully capable of.

https://www.firsttutors.com/uk/tutor/joseph.english.psychology.philosophy-critical-thinking.religious-studies/

https://www.superprof.co.uk/joseph-english-teacher-and-writer-twenty-years-teaching-experience-proven-track-record-enhanced-dbs-check-the-update-service.html

My books have helped over 6000 readers and I am grateful to you for purchasing my book and to all who allow me to help them succeed. I hope to be able to help you further in the future.

Best wishes,

Joseph

P.S. For all professional enquiries, I can be contacted via email at Joseph@agradeexams.com

Printed in Great Britain
by Amazon